Praise Him!

WITH SONG

HYMNS – VOLUME ONE

(MEDIUM LOW VOICE)

T0058911

CONTENTS

EDITED BY DAN RODOWICZ
DESIGN BY DIANE JACOBS
ENGRAVED BY JOE COX

PRAISE HIM! WITH SONG

KMP9702 (Book only)   KMP9702CD (Book/CD pack)   KMP9702CDL (Compact Disk only)

Keveren
MUSIC PRESS

EXCLUSIVELY DISTRIBUTED BY

HAL•LEONARD®
CORPORATION

7777 W. BLUEMOUND RD. P.O. BOX 13819 MILWAUKEE, WI 53213

FOREWORD...

One of the greatest joys I experience as a musician is accompanying vocalists. There is a special bond between singer and pianist as they collaborate in bringing words and music to life. The timeless texts in this collection are arranged in the tradition of the artsong, with familiar and newly-composed melodies joining together to praise Him with song.

This book is dedicated with love to all the talented and dedicated vocalists with whom I have served over the years. Thank you for sharing your gift!

In His Service,

Phillip Keveren

Phillip Keveren

Amazing Grace

Traditional American Melody
Text by John Newton (stanzas 1-4)
and John P. Rees (stanza 5)
Arr. by Phillip Keveren

Vocal Range

Lightly, with motion

mp

with pedal

poco rit. mf p a tempo

mp

A-maz — ing — grace! how — sweet the sound _____ That — saved a ____

* *Optional notes extend range*

cures. He will my shield and por - tion be As long as life en - dures. Through man - y

Slower

rit. *mf with passion*

mf solidly

dan - gers, toils and snares, I have al - read - y come; 'Tis

(L.H.)

sun, We've no less

days to sing God's praise Than

when we first be - gun.

Come, Thou Fount of Every Blessing

Traditional American Melody
Text by Robert Robinson
Arr. by Phillip Keveren

Teach me _ some me - lo - dious son - net, Sung by _ flam - ing tongues a - bove; Praise His name — I'm fixed up - on it, Name of God's re - deem - ing love.

Hith - er - to Thy love has blest me; Thou hast

Somewhat freely, with despair

Thee: Prone to wan - der, Lord, I feel it, Prone to leave the God I

love; Here's my

heart, O take and seal it; Seal it for Thy courts a -

bove.

A Mighty Fortress Is Our God

Vocal Range

Music and text by Martin Luther
Arr. by Phillip Keveren

seek to make us woe. _____ His craft and pow'r are great, _____ And, armed with cru-el hate, On earth is not His e - qual.

D.S. al Coda

Coda

ing.

age the same, _____ And He must win the bat - tle. A might - y for - tress is ___ our God, _____ A bul - wark nev - er fail - ing. _____

Come, Ye Thankful People, Come

Music by George J. Elvey
Text by Henry Alford
Arr. by Phillip Keveren

Immortal, Invisible

Traditional Welsh Hymn Melody
Text by Walter Chalmers Smith
(based on 1Timothy 1:17)
Arr. by Phillip Keveren

Vocal Range

Maestoso

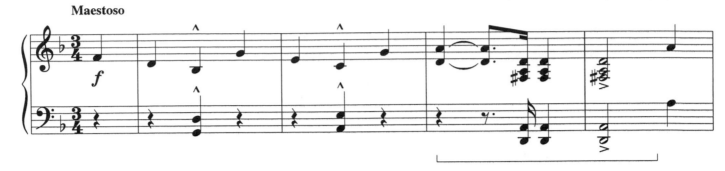

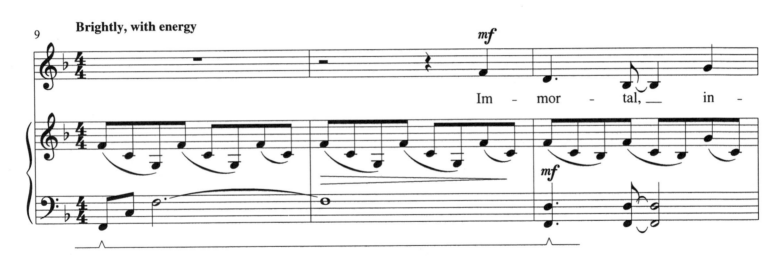

Let Us Break Bread Together

Traditional Spiritual
Arr. by Phillip Keveren

fall on my knees with my face to the ris - ing

sun, O____ Lord, have mer-cy on me.

Let us

praise God to - geth-er on our knees;_____ Let us

O for a Thousand Tongues

Music by Carl G. Glazer
Text by Charles Wesley
Arr. by Phillip Keveren

The Old Rugged Cross

Music and text by George Bennard
Arr. by Phillip Keveren

Vocal Range

I will cling to the old rug - ged cross, _____

And ex - change it some day for a crown. _____

To the old rug - ged cross I will ev - er be

Were You There?

Traditional Spiritual
Arr. by Phillip Keveren

Were you there when they nailed Him to the tree? Were you there when they laid Him in the tomb? Were you there when they laid Him in the tomb?

God Be with You

Music by William G. Tomer
Text by Jeremiah E. Rankin
Arr. by Phillip Keveren

Vocal Range

About the "Praise Him!" Series . . .

"Let everything that has breath praise the Lord . . ."

The traditional hymns and contemporary and original songs in the "Praise Him!" series give voice to all the musicians in God's kingdom.

THE CREATIVE ARRANGEMENTS IN THIS SERIES ARE:

- available as Piano Solos and as Vocal and Instrumental Solos with piano accompaniment.

- written in a contemporary style that reflects the refinements of the classical tradition.

- appropriate for church services or recitals.

- playable by accomplished musicians with minimal preparation or by developing intermediate musicians with a reasonable amount of practice.

- available with CD accompaniments ideal for rehearsal or performance.